SIX STEPS
to Workplace Happiness

MARK PRICE

www.measuringworkplacehappiness.com

STO
PUBL
An im
David Fic

Published in Great Britain in 2017 by Stour Publishing
An imprint of David Fickling Books

31 Beaumont Street,
Oxford,
OX1 2NP

www.davidficklingbooks.com

British Library Cataloguing-in-Publication Data
A catalogue record for this book is available on
request from the British Library

ISBN 978 1 910989 92 0

Typeset in Minion Pro 11.5/17

Printed and bound in Great Britain by Clays Ltd, St Ives plc

CONTENTS

The Machine

by Mark Price

*In the beginning was the idea and the idea was good, so
good it became a machine.*

*The machine only exists to make money for those
who own it.*
*The machine doesn't care about the consequences
of its actions if it makes more money.*
The machine that hesitates is consumed by another.
*The machine doesn't mind being consumed if it
makes more money for the owners.*
*The machine demands consistency, order,
uniformity, process and efficiency.*
*The machine keeps making new rules and ways to
check them.*
The machine doesn't trust.
The machine gives orders, but doesn't explain.
The machine talks to you, but you can't talk to it.
The machine has to grow.
The machine demands more each year.
*The machine that breaks down has its broken parts reused
or discarded.*

There is a different way.

Introduction

There are the six steps that drive the happiness of employees:

Step One: Reward and recognition
Pay is important in any job, but linking it to recognition is a powerful motivator.

Step Two: Information sharing
An open, transparent culture ensures widespread understanding of objectives.

Step Three: Empowerment
Once employees know what needs to be done, if you empower them they'll make intelligent suggestions and be more committed to the best way forward.

Step Four: Well-being

A happy, healthy workforce is better equipped to do business.

Step Five: Instilling pride

Pride in the workplace and its status in society adds to fulfilment.

Step Six: Job satisfaction

A culture of trust and respect engages on a personal level and encourages a stronger bond.

These elements control our sense of happiness in what we do each working day and, in turn, ensure we give the best we have to get the job done. If you visit measuringworkplacehappiness.com you or your organisation can get both quantitative and qualitative measurements of happiness.

For more than three decades I worked for The John Lewis Partnership whose supreme purpose was the happiness of its employees, or Partners as they are called, not maximising shareholder returns or being customer-centric, but putting employee well-being first.

Over the last ten years, as a business leader and government minister, I have heard increasing calls for a more 'inclusive capitalism' and a 'fairer form of capitalism' as a response to the financial crisis of 2008 and the perceived and real excesses of capitalism. There is a widely held belief that there is too large a gap between the haves and the have-nots, that jobs are being lost to technology and cheaper labour, and that as a result people are working harder to stand still, and that big business is acting unfairly, and that institutions and governments are failing the people.

To my mind, inclusive capitalism means engaging employees more in their organisation's success, and in so doing, more fairly balancing rewards and responsibility, not just for the employees' benefit, but also for that of customers and local communities as well as shareholders and business leaders. This is sustainable capitalism.

I believe there is a moral as well as an economic imperative for employees to be more engaged in their organisations – any organisation. The straightforward message is that if you focus first and foremost on your employees' well-being and happiness, your organisation will do better and society will be better off too. That is because workplace happiness is derived from a sense of ownership and control and feeling positive about the environment in which you work. It drives increased productivity and commitment, which drives increased customer satisfaction, which drives increased profitability from which shareholders and society benefits.

The lessons I draw from my experience are summarised here, but are set out in more detail in my book *Fairness For All*. In it, through numerous examples, I have tried to show that elements of the JLP model can translate very successfully elsewhere however your business or organisation is constructed. If employee happiness is the objective, it is possible to create a sense of ownership and responsibility around a business in a range of ways. Individuals who feel they have more power over their working life, well-being and environment will take more responsibility for the success of their employer. The endgame should be a more engaged society that promotes greater happiness, collective endeavour and a fairer sharing of success.

Step One

Reward and recognition

Well thought-out reward and recognition initiatives, coupled with a conducive working environment, help create sustainable long-term teams, and businesses that are beneficial to employees, the community and society as a whole.

Key Points
- That everyone in an organisation enjoys the rewards of success.
- If you're not paying a fair salary no amount of recognition for a job well done will be enough to make employees forget they are not being paid enough.
- Your pay scale has to meet expectations and encourage discretionary effort.

(In The John Lewis Partnership all individuals are paid the market rate for their job, and as much above as can be justified by their performance.)

But to maximise employees' performance and pay it is important to recognise you need the following three things from those managing:

- Leadership – which is consistent, and shows a sincere interest in the team.
- Managers – who are consistent, impartial and honest and willing to provide appropriate feedback and coaching.
- Goals – of both business and individuals should be clearly and explicitly understood and expressed and whenever possible set by those delivering them so that they are truly owned.

In the Partnership, each Partner is guaranteed an equal percentage share in the profits, from the Chairman to the part-time student. As set out in the constitution, the highest-paid director is not allowed to earn more than seventy-five times as much as a non-management employee. But fairer sharing in The John Lewis Partnership goes beyond pay and bonus. There are generous subsidies for Partners to enjoy their hobbies, a market-leading pension scheme to reward longevity of service, and holiday centres for employees to use. These are all designed to recognise and reward the team as well as individual merit.

Research and experience has shown me that recognising a individual's performance with a thank you, a note of congratulation or small gift of acknowledgement, is a powerful motivator. It says good work has been noticed throughout the year, not just at an annual appraisal. It builds bonds and trust and increases engagement.

NOTES:

Step Two

Information sharing

- Sharing information is the most important and difficult element of achieving an engaged workforce.
- Not sharing information makes employees feel an unimportant part of the business. Engagement and commitment is eroded by this.
- The closed-door approach doesn't just have a negative impact on engagement, it can directly impact on decision-making, and therefore profitability and success.

We all need to have a realistic and well-sourced view of the organisations where we work, regardless of whether we are the chief executive or work on the shop floor. The level of detail in which we receive it may be different, but information forms the basis of the decisions we make every day.

Key Points

- A culture where information is freely available is fundamental to achieving each of the six steps to happiness.
- Information is the basis of democratic participation.
- If you are a business that wants to get the best out of individuals on the team, openness is key.
- It is impossible to give people a greater say, or to demonstrate they have a share in the commercial success of your organisation, without equipping them with the full facts.
- You need to share with the employees as much knowledge as you are able, in order to give them the context of what you are trying to achieve.

This doesn't mean a bunch of missives that come down from Head Office saying: this is our strategy. No, employees at all levels need a genuine overview of what is going on in their area and elsewhere. If employees understand the business, its strategy, how it is doing and who are its customers and competitors, they will make it stronger. Knowledge will enable employees to take an influential role in important decisions. Individuals on the team will have valuable input on working methods and work together to coordinate their efforts.

None of this means that those at the top have less information or knowledge, simply that overall the business becomes flatter and information is spread throughout the organisation. It makes for effective decision-making and involvement at all levels. But it requires managers to behave differently: accept and welcome challenge, be collaborative and thoughtful, explain actions and embrace good ideas, no matter where they come from.

NOTES:

Step Three

Empowerment

The aim of any business must surely be to make its employees feel empowered, and this means:

- making them a key part of the decision-making process
- listening to their ideas
- integrating their suggestions to build and refine your strategy.

Our personal experiences inevitably bring us all to different solutions and ways of achieving our objectives, but only by listening to all views can the best outcome be reached. Nobody is perfect, but a team can be.

Key Points

- Reward your team by giving them freedom,

power, trust, autonomy and encouragement
– they will be more productive and feel more
responsible because they feel more in control.

- Allow employees to make decisions on their own,
  and let them experience the success that follows.
  This helps them feel valued and rewarded – they
  associate success with their own abilities and
  efforts, which in turn motivates them to strive for
  more in future tasks.

By keeping teams informed and empowering them
to use their knowledge, individuals will add value by
doing more complicated tasks, better managing and
controlling themselves, coordinating their work with
other employees, suggesting ideas about better ways
to work, and developing new products and ways to
serve customers.

Engaged employees boost productivity because
they direct their energy towards the right tasks and
outcomes. The only way this can happen is if you give
them the knowledge and equipment to do so and the
confidence to use their own judgement.

A practical framework of meetings, systems and support is needed to help employees to do the following:

1. Feel valued – If individuals feel appreciated and listened to – as well as appropriately rewarded – they will give more of themselves.

2. Freely voice ideas – Be receptive to new ideas, no individual has a monopoly on them, and be prepared to engage in a two-way debate.

3. Reject conflict – Accept and acknowledge that everyone will have different viewpoints and so regular, good-quality feedback is accepted as an important part of improving performance levels. Quickly acknowledge that everyone is working to the same end. Conflict is thus minimised and time is not wasted.

4. Work as a team – When it is well known that all experiences and skills are recognised and encouraged, people have positive feelings

about the job and their colleagues. There is a drive to achieve on a personal level as well as to support each other.

5. Manage differences – Actively seek a diverse team, welcome and acknowledge the differences to help build the best outcomes and create an atmosphere of collaboration. By doing this you ensure that differences are not allowed to get in the way, or to become a simmering source of conflict. In fact, the team comes to see differing views as a strength.

6. Take ownership – By creating a no-blame environment where people are encouraged to talk openly, rather than moan about things behind closed doors, people are more willing to take joint responsibility with management.

Leaders who try to enforce and police everything stifle collaboration. Setting out best practice and guidelines is fine, but it's just as important to give employees the tools and let them get on with what they need to do. In this approach, leaders are coaches and skilled communicators. They focus on creating a culture for people to give their best. Leaders are still accountable, but through serving their teams, rather than the other way around. Leaders see the value of decentralisation rather than building an ever-controlling centre.

NOTES:

STEP FOUR

WELL-BEING

Health and well-being can be broken down into three key areas:

- Physical
- Emotional
- Financial.

By addressing all three, employers will improve engagement levels and productivity.

There is a growing body of evidence to support the idea that well-being is an essential aspect of employee engagement. It leads to improved production, lower rates of absence and stress, and higher levels of motivation. In other words, employee health and well-being has become a hard economic factor. A few years ago a PricewaterhouseCoopers report estimated that sick leave cost the UK £29 billion annually. Other reports suggest that's around 130 million sick days. Happy workplaces have lower levels of absence because people are engaged, and engagement strengthens well-being.

None of the actions or strategies outlined can be effective unless an employer creates the right environment in which employees can make informed, well-thought-through and prudent choices. To do this, your teams need to be relaxed, healthy and feel comfortable in their environment.

At the heart of well-being are relationships based on mutual trust and respect that managers have with their team members, and individuals have with one another, so they are able to proactively and reactively spot and discuss any concerns they may have and get the timely help they need. Listening to employees and responding to their anxieties plays a crucial role too.

Key Points
- Attending to health and well-being creates a virtuous circle of benefits.
- Not only is there a strong correlation between

pastoral care and employee engagement, the two are mutually reinforcing.

- Healthy employees are more committed, and committed employees are more healthy.

The focus here needs to be on the long term. Businesses that pursue a strategy of engagement in the short term, without thinking about well-being, won't be able to sustain the strategy. There will be higher absence rates and higher employee turnover, which will be ultimately self-defeating.

NOTES:

STEP FIVE

INSTILLING PRIDE

Employees who love what they do and feel proud of where they work will speak openly and positively about it to colleagues, potential employees, customers and people in their community. When people ask that inevitable, getting-to-know-you question of 'where do you work?', you'll hear the pleasure in their voice when they reply. Instilling such pride is not just about stirring speeches, sharing growth figures, or saying a few well-placed thank yous.

Key Points:
- Instilling pride centres on having a purpose and helping everyone see that what they do each day is worthwhile.

- How your business interacts with the wider world is part of instilling such pride.
- People want to work for an organisation that cares about how it impacts on society.
- If people feel they make a difference, it leaves them more fulfilled.

Community Social Responsibility (CSR) plays a crucial role in employee engagement, with all the advantages of increased productivity, innovation and staff retention that goes with it. Plus, it affords any company the opportunity to bring about a positive change on a mass scale. It doesn't just make sense for the business and your employees, it also has the potential to significantly impact on wider society and to change people's lives for the better.

CSR initiatives attract people and keep them engaged. They help create a positive working environment where people work hard because they want to, not because they have to. People are motivated by a sense of achievement and by doing something worthwhile. Being able to contribute to a cause while at work improves commitment to both the core job and to the company as a whole.

NOTES:

STEP SIX

JOB SATISFACTION

There are many elements to feeling satisfied at work, but time and again, two key reasons are cited:

- Personal development
- The strength of your relationship with the line manager.

We have nothing of greater value than our people. A high level of employee engagement is the key to unlock organisational success. Happy employees equal a high-performing, successful and long-lasting business. But what makes people tick on a personal level? In other words, what makes workers happy and satisfied at work? More importantly, what can business leaders do about it?

Research shows that the two biggest drivers of satisfaction are:

- 'Respectful treatment'
- 'Trust between employees and senior management'.

A poor relationship with your manager is often cited as the number-one reason for leaving an organisation, no matter how great the brand. Forget all the perks, incentives, reviews and motivational tactics: treating people with humanity is what really counts. Satisfaction is principally about what companies are doing at a personal level to make people's lives better.

Key Points

- Developing a culture of trust and respect and giving workers opportunities to learn and develop will make all the difference.
- If you want to create deep-seated loyalty among your team, you need to show them you care and let them have defined autonomy.
- It is impossible for employees to have pride in what they are doing if they are constantly being told what to do and how to do it.

When employees feel that their company appreciates them, they exert discretionary effort to make their workplace an even better place to be. They willingly contribute to their firm's continuing success. They'll do whatever is necessary to get the job done and get it right. The resultant deep emotional attachment and loyalty to their employer means they stay for longer. Add all these elements together and it creates an energised workplace.

Personal engagement starts right at the beginning, with your recruitment process. Getting the right fit is very important. Look for people with the right attitude, who talk positively about challenges and outcomes. Stress that the interview is not to test their technical skills, which will be clear already, but a chance for them to be open about how they work so that you can weigh up whether they will complement the team and be happy.

Employees must believe that what they do complements the greater whole. There are real benefits to be gained from spending more time showing employees how their individual contributions help their company succeed. Whether it is someone in purchasing who finds a way to improve the quality of products, or a cashier that sees to it a customer leaves with a smile on their face, it pays to communicate that these actions are crucial to corporate success. Be sure to celebrate successes and achievements. It doesn't take much to recognise a job well done, but it immediately creates strong bonds and a sense of pride. Everyone needs to feel valued and to be provided with the opportunity to make a difference through their work. It is an ongoing process where contributions are regularly noticed and appreciated. People thrive on praise. Equally, individuals should feel confident they are in an environment that constantly promotes learning, creativity and growth.

Instead of discarding people when the organisation needs a new skill-set, retrain them. Demonstrate that you value their previous commitment and experience. Job security and stability are hugely valuable drivers in the way people feel about their employer. Employees who feel their positions are insecure will inevitably put in an effort to impress, but at the same time will be looking for the life-raft of alternative employment should things not work out well. They'll feel undervalued and disconnected from their organisation. If, however, your company's goal is to provide sustained employment through constant retraining and development because you value longevity, the atmosphere and outcomes will be distinctly different.

Being in a rewarding and satisfying relationship means both sides taking notice of what the other has to say. No one wants to work in a business where they simply survive from day to day. We all want to feel excited about our working day and look forward to a bright future. Businesses will only ever achieve their full potential with the full support of their teams, through their employees sense of self-worth and maximised potential.

NOTES:

DIVERSITY

There is another factor that is important to workplace happiness, and that is diversity. I'm not talking here about gender, race or sexual orientation diversity, but diversity of views, knowledge and experience. Diversity has become a numbers game, all about hitting quotas and targets in order to present equality in the workplace. But the real benefit of diversity runs deeper than that and is imperative for commercial success, high-performing teams and workplace engagement.

You see, to be at their best, teams need the broadest range of experience in order to make high-quality decisions that benefit ALL employees, customers and shareholders. From the outset, the founder of The John Lewis Partnership, Spedan Lewis, set out to be an equal opportunities employer and put that down in his written constitution. He saw the huge talent and diversity of thinking that came from recruiting people from different backgrounds, and he developed a culture where their views were freely and openly heard and appreciated. To accommodate different cultural and practical needs he was prepared to be flexible in setting working arrangements. Recent examples of this philosophy include job-shares for branch managers with caring responsibilities and embracing mobile technology so managers can work from home as well as in the shop or office.

It is because it makes your business better and happier that you should recruit from the broadest possible range of backgrounds, not because you have a quota to hit. And to make that work, managers need to explain that differences are welcomed because they are to everyone's benefit. Once diversity of thought, experience and background has been achieved, the key is to nurture and encourage it.

NOTES:

Measurement

www.measuringworkplaceengagement.com

If you believe that workplace happiness is key to sustained commercial success you will want to measure it. To begin, there are a few measures that are relatively easy to collect. Four are key:

- Staff turnover
- Sickness absence
- Internal promotions
- Longevity.

Averages are often the preserve of the ill-informed and lazy, as while there is some advantage to understanding these figures on a company-wide basis, the real benefit comes in being able to break them down by department or manager. You see, employees will normally leave a manager who doesn't give them what they need, no matter how good the business or brand. As set out in the chapter on satisfaction, good line-management is key to securing engagement.

An employee survey, such as the one that can be found at www.measuringworkplaceengagement.com, whether annual or more frequent, can then add colour to the employment statistics. To my mind, the key to such an approach is not to use it to beat line management, but instead to inform and guide on how to improve staff turnover, sickness absence, longevity, etc. over time. Surveys are best, therefore, when consistent over a number of years, so as to monitor progress and build around the six areas crucial to achieve engagement, namely reward and recognition, information, empowerment, well-being, worthwhile work, and satisfaction. Within each of these areas businesses will want to choose questions that are appropriate for them, but you could begin with a ten-question survey as straightforward as the following:

1. Do you feel appropriately rewarded for your work?

2. Do you feel recognised when you do something well?

3. Do you feel as though you have enough information to do your job well?

4. Do you feel empowered to make decisions?

5. Do you feel trusted to make decisions?

6. Do you feel the business cares for your well-being?

7. Do you feel you do something worthwhile?

8. Do you feel you are treated with respect?

9. Do you feel that you are being developed?

10. Do you feel satisfied in your work?

This sort of survey, scored on a 1–10, low to high basis, and coupled with employee comments, will provide the basis for building programmes to increase employee happiness and engagement. You can visit www.measuringworkplacehappiness.com to see how you and your company score.

NOTES:

CONCLUSION

The Six Steps to Happiness is not one-size-fits-all. There will be aspects already well developed in some businesses, while other firms will feel only some elements are right for them. It very much depends upon your culture and what you do. Only you can say what works best for your organisation and how you choose to populate this framework. Each one of these steps makes a substantial difference, but the decision is yours on how important it is to make your employees feel better informed in your organisation, or the benefits of giving them more power and influence, or whether well-being should be the top of your priority list. I would very much hope that after reading this book managers will find ways to show individuals on their team that what they are doing is worthwhile, and help them have satisfying jobs.

In the end, it all boils down to inputs and outputs.

The prevailing thought in recent years has been that if you focus on making profit above all else, you get the best output. My response would be: but for whom and for how long? What Spedan Lewis realised a very long time ago is that if you look after your people you will get great output. Happiness is an input, not an output. We should be starting by trying to make people happy. If we get this right, everything else will follow: wealth will be more widely shared, the nation will become more productive and our communities will be better off. What I am calling for is for people to be more engaged in the workplace, to better share responsibility and rewards, and to be engaged in the delivery of public services and in our democracy. In short, I am calling for a more engaged society that promotes greater happiness, collective endeavour and fairer sharing of success.

What is being advocated here is more than making the workplace, or even the world, a bit happier and a bit more decent. It's an argument in favour of a fairer form of capitalism because for capitalism to survive it needs to be more inclusive. Capitalism is not an end in its own right, it needs to be part of a value system. Smart societies cannot be created without fairness, equality and enfranchisement, and businesses have a crucial role to play. Society, quite rightly, expects a lot in return from business for the privileges it is afforded. Now is the time to deliver the goods.

NOTES: